Clint Black

Looking for Christmas

Editor: Carol Cuellar

CONTENTS

Looking for Christmas

Words and Music by
CLINT BLACK

The Birth of the King

Words and Music by
CLINT BLACK

Verse 2:

Frankincense, gold and myrrh honor the Savior's birth.
The highest praise on earth,
The angels will sing of Him, the Trinity begins,
Voices will ring amen, the birth of the King.

Chorus 2:

Jesus, Joseph and Mary of Israel,
Isaiah's miracle augured befell,
The coming of Christ as the star from the east will tell,
The first Noel, our Lord Emmanuel.

Christmas for Every Boy and Girl

Words and Music by
CLINT BLACK

Verse:

The Coolest Pair

The Coolest Pair - 4 - 1
PF9550

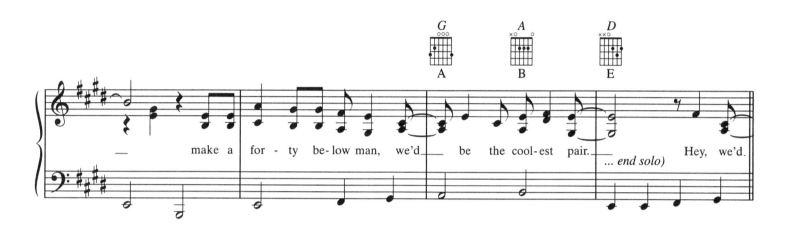

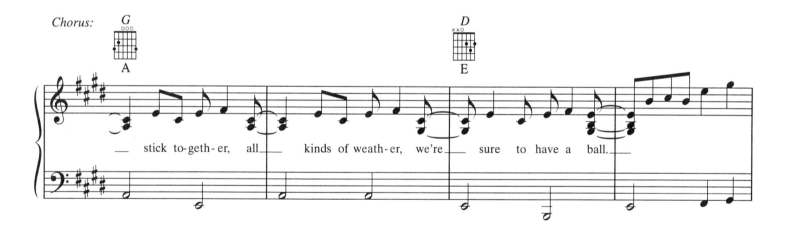

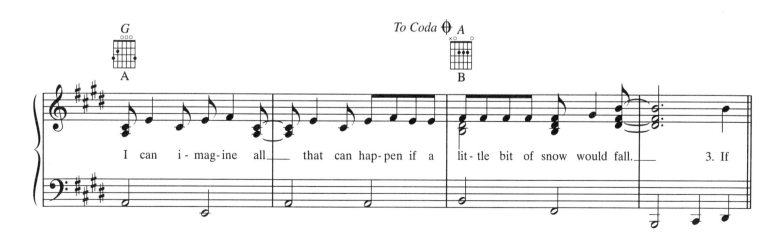

The Coolest Pair - 4 - 2
PF9550

The Finest Gift

Words and Music by
CLINT BLACK and HAYDEN NICHOLAS

shop all o - ver town, _____ turn the gift shops up - side down _____
ev - 'ry - thing _____ you'll see _____ scat - tered un - der - neath _____ our tree. _____

The Finest Gift - 4 - 1
PF9550

23

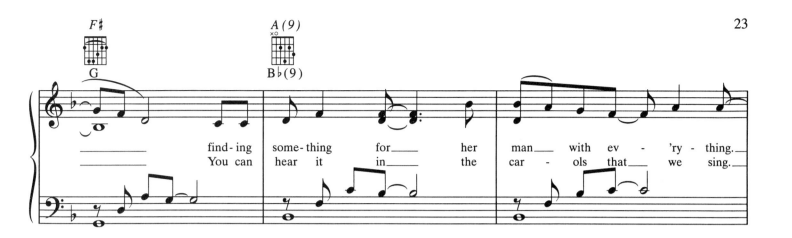

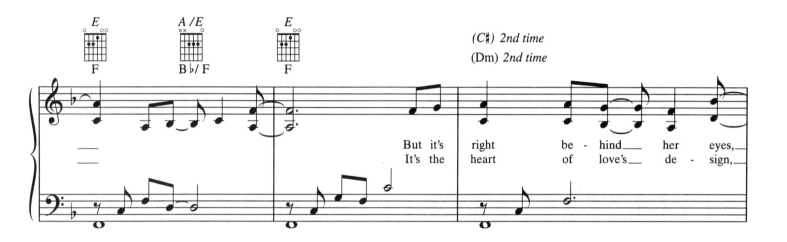

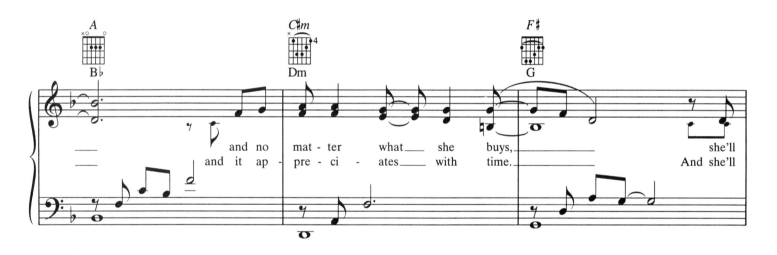

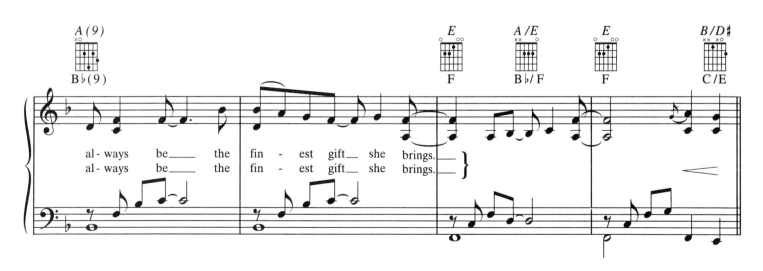

The Finest Gift - 4 - 2
PF9550

Slow as Christmas

Words and Music by
CLINT BLACK and
HAYDEN NICHOLAS

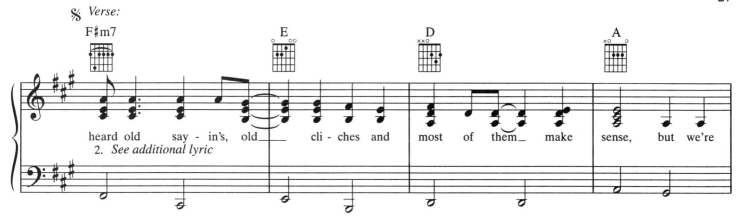

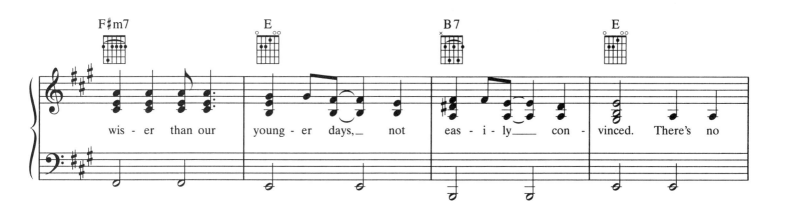

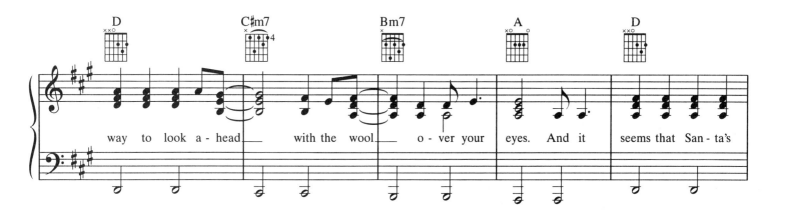

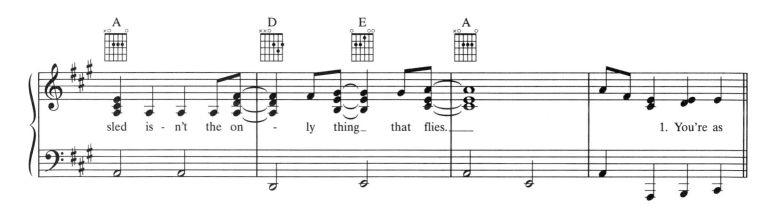

Chorus:

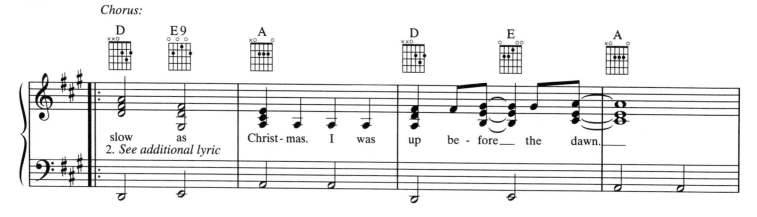

slow as Christ-mas. I was up be-fore_ the dawn._
2. *See additional lyric*

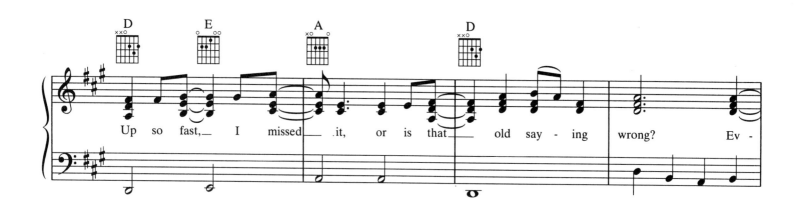

Up so fast,_ I missed_ it, or is that_ old say - ing wrong? Ev -

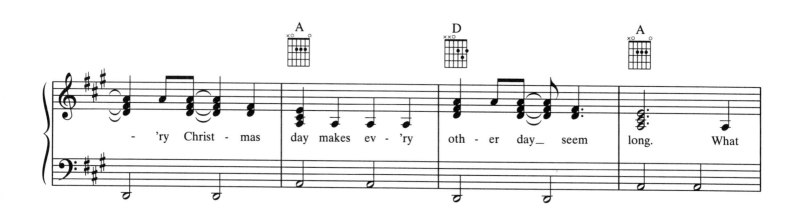

- 'ry Christ - mas day makes ev - 'ry oth - er day_ seem long. What

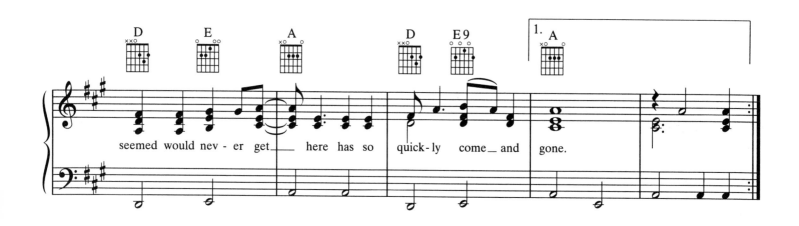

seemed would nev - er get_ here has so quick-ly come_ and gone.

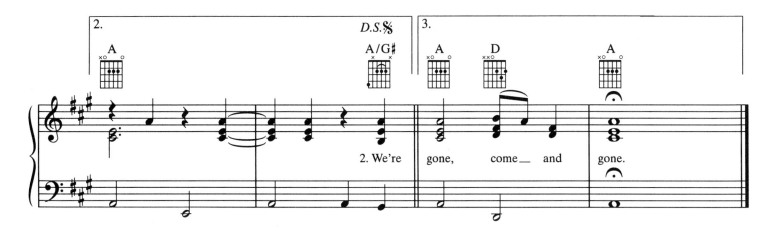

Verse 2:

We're bringing in another year. Let's throw that old one back.
With my new train, I'll be the engineer and hurry down the track.
While I know that time is standin' still, I hear that old cliche,
And I'm more convinced it does until that one December day.
(To Chorus:)

Chorus 2:

When I'm as slow as Christmas.
I'll be up before the dawn.
I'm not gonna miss this;
I know that old sayin's wrong.
Every Christmas day makes every other day seem long.
What seemed would never get here has so
Quickly come and gone, come and gone.

'Til Santa's Gone (Milk and Cookies)

Words and Music by
CLINT BLACK, HAYDEN NICHOLAS and
SHAKE RUSSELL

Verse 3:

But could there be something I might have missed?
I had quite a few things on my list.
I hope he can fit it all under that Christmas tree.

Verse 4:
(Instrumental solo ad lib.)
(To Chorus 2:)

Chorus 2:

Sneak a peek down the hall;
I've gotta check now, I don't recall,
The milk and cookies.
I think I'm sure I've got it all,
The stockings hung along the wall;
Ain't got a chimney. *(To Bridge 2:)*

Bridge 2:

Close my eyes and concentrate;
I've got to sleep now, it's gettin' late.
All night long I lie awake 'til Santa's gone.
I just can't wait, I just can't wait, I just can't wait.

Under the Mistletoe

Moderate jazz swing ♩ = 120

Words and Music by
CLINT BLACK

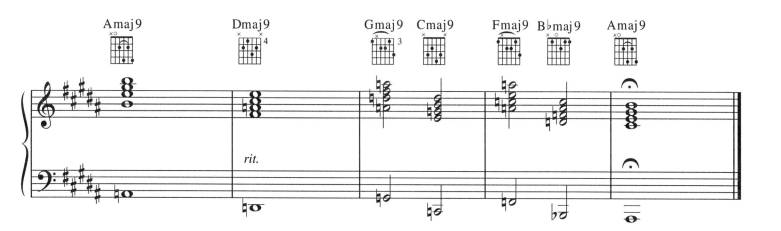

Verse 2:

That lovely holiday dish made a mess of me.
If love is this, it's my favorite recipe,
The kind I'd fix to remind the rest of me
There's room to grow under the mistletoe.

Verse 3:

Will I be dismissed as a Christmas wanna be
With a Christmas list that insists I've gotta be
Hugged and kissed by this sweetness in front of me
On Christmas night and every night?

Verse 4:

Just right here in the doorway where they found us;
They'd like to leave, but there's no way around us.
I believe there's a spell that bound us.
I've gotta know; is it only the mistletoe?
(To Chorus:)

The Kid

Words and Music by
CLINT BLACK, HAYDEN NICHOLAS
and MERLE HAGGARD

Slowly ♩ = 72

Verse:

1. Last night I dreamed I was ___ a kid a-gain, ___ all the
2. *See additional lyrics*

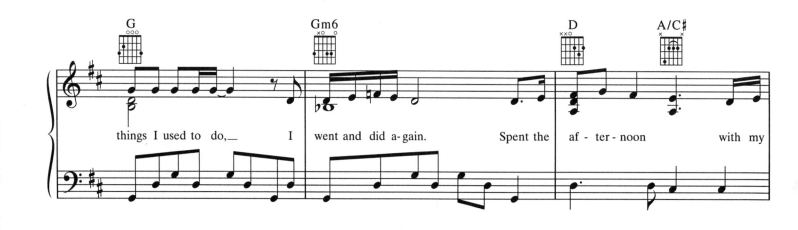

things I used to do, ___ I went and did a-gain. Spent the af-ter-noon with my

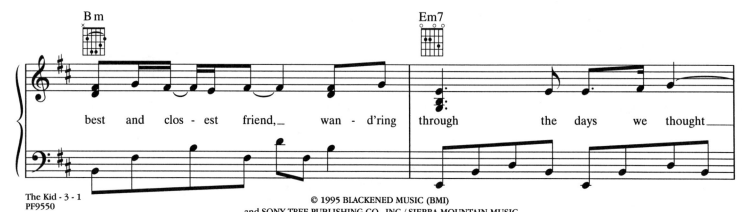

best and clos-est friend, ___ wan-d'ring through the days we thought ___

The Kid - 3 - 1
PF9550

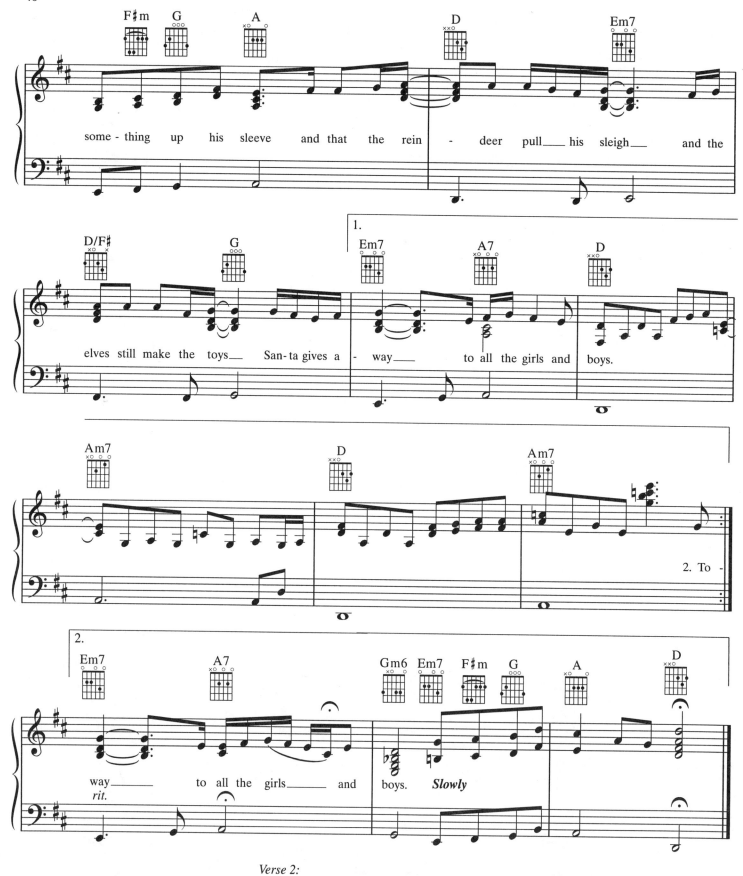

Verse 2:

Tonight I'll climb back in that bed again,
Try to live out my the dreams inside my head again.
After Christmas Eve with my best and closest friend,
Who still believes the World's Greatest Dad just tucked him in.
And I know that he'll be looking out for Santa Claus,
And I'm sure beyond a doubt, he'll overlook the flaws
That will grow inside until it hides
This perfect little boy inside the man.
(To Chorus:)